Avrum R. Goldstein
DMD, FRCD (C)

A DENTIST'S GUIDE TO SUCCESS!

A handbook that will show you the keys to reducing stress, improving productivity, and ultimately finding success and happiness in dental practice

outskirts
press

A Dentist's Guide To Success!
A handbook that will show you the keys to reducing stress, improving productivity, and ultimately finding success and happiness in dental practice
All Rights Reserved.
Copyright © 2019 Avrum R. Goldstein DMD, FRCD (C)
v5.0

The opinions expressed in this manuscript are solely the opinions of the author and do not represent the opinions or thoughts of the publisher. The author has represented and warranted full ownership and/or legal right to publish all the materials in this book.

This book may not be reproduced, transmitted, or stored in whole or in part by any means, including graphic, electronic, or mechanical without the express written consent of the publisher except in the case of brief quotations embodied in critical articles and reviews.

Outskirts Press, Inc.
http://www.outskirtspress.com

ISBN: 978-1-9772-1702-8

Cover Photo © 2019 Avrum R. Goldstein DMD, FRCD (C). All rights reserved - used with permission.

Outskirts Press and the "OP" logo are trademarks belonging to Outskirts Press, Inc.

PRINTED IN THE UNITED STATES OF AMERICA

"No matter how good your clinical skills, if your patients don't trust you and your staff doesn't respect you, you will be neither productive nor happy in dental practice."

The world of medicine has changed dramatically during the past 50 years. Personalized care typified by warmth and spending time with patients has been replaced with a much more structured, mechanized approach. Doctors spend less time with patients and auxiliaries have taken over many of the duties once performed by physicians. Without getting into the reasons why this has occurred, it has resulted in a very different type of doctor-patient relationship. We used to know our doctors and trust them, and they used to know us. This type of doctor-patient relationship was, to a large degree, a product of the time spent together. The more time spent with our physician, the better we knew each other, and the better we knew each other, the more our trust grew.

We are in a new era of medical care where physician remuneration limits the time they can spend with patients. However, dentistry is not in the same position. We can spend time with patients, earn their trust and still make a handsome living. In fact, dentists are in a unique position to create the type of bond with patients that was once typical of the physician-patient relationship.

I would suggest that creating a trusting relationship with a patient is particularly important when it comes to dentistry. Many of the dental problems we identify in our patients are at an early stage, before symptoms have developed. We know that if these problems are treated in a timely way, we will not only prevent them from becoming more complex and costly problems, we will prevent our patients from experiencing pain and suffering.

Symptoms reinforce the need for treatment as soon as possible. However, in the absence of symptoms, we are relying on our patient's trust to believe what we are telling them is true, and that this will encourage them to pursue treatment when we recommend it. There is a truism, which is almost universal: *"It will never be easier or cheaper to fix than it is today!"* The key to providing the best possible care for our patients is to gain their trust.

In addition to the relationships we form with our patients, relationships with staff, colleagues, community and families shape our lives and contribute to our overall experience as dentists. Come with me to explore these avenues of productivity, stress reduction and enjoyment.

As the dentist and owner of the practice, no matter what happens, it is your fault!

Accepting responsibility for your own shortcomings, your staff's conduct or your patient's behavior is the first step in creating a productive, respectful and enjoyable place to work.

Let's say an instrument breaks during a procedure.... did it break because you were applying too much force? Did it break because you were rushing? Did it break because it was worn out, but you were delaying its replacement as a cost-saving measure? Those are all within your control.... it is your fault the instrument broke. Accept responsibility for it! Learn from it!

Your staff is not behaving the way you would like them to (how they are treating the patients, talking about personal things in front of the patient, not passing instruments carefully, not preparing a room correctly, not mixing impression material properly, not cleaning a room properly, not practicing the highest standards of infection control, etc.....)- these are all your fault. It is your responsibility to educate your staff and monitor their performance.

If their performance falls below the standards you have created for your office, it is your job to reeducate them. If this continually fails, it is your job to replace them, because they will bring down the performance of every other staff member, not to mention making it impossible to maintain excellent standards in your office and meet your professional goals. Their behavior will also negatively affect the quality of care you deliver and patient confidence in your office, and destroy the respect you have been so valiantly trying to create.

If your relationship with your colleagues is fractious, it is likely your fault. Have you shown your colleagues respect? Have you reached out to them to discuss differences of opinion? We will discuss this in more detail in a little while.

What is a new patient?

It is important to remember that when you see a patient for the first time, that patient is new to you, not new to dentistry. Unless the patient has recently moved, it is quite likely that the patient is in your office because he or she is unhappy with his or her previous dentist. Was it quality of care? Convenience? Pain associated with treatment? Cost of treatment? Interpersonal relationships with the dentist or office staff? For whatever reason, you have a one-time opportunity to make a first impression, and that impression will have as much to do with your communication skills as it will the patient's treatment needs. Your ability to create the trust necessary to foster a positive dentist-patient relationship will determine whether or not your new patient will become someone else's new patient in the near future.

Relationships with patients:

Patients don't care how much you know, until they know how much you care!

Our relationships with our patients are complex. Most patients come to us with a history of dental care, and this history is often filled with pain and fear, and as a result, less than ideal dentistry or neglect. When we examine patients and find substandard care, missing teeth, active infection or signs of neglect, we are often looking at a patient who has avoided or declined dental care because of their fear. How can we succeed where others have failed? How can we overcome a lifetime history of bad dentistry as a result of fear and neglect to make patients comfortable in our chair and amenable to our recommendations? How can we create the trust that is required to change our patient's perceptions and comfort level, so they will have the same goals for their oral health that we have for them?

It doesn't happen in one visit. There are many years of dental experiences that need to be overcome. It requires an investment on our part of time, patience, education and understanding. Gaining a patient's trust is the first and most important step in building a long-term relationship, and this is most effectively done by understanding how to talk to patients, how to educate patients, by providing only the highest standard of care, and by structuring their treatment in such a way that you plan for the long term, not short-term gain. Furthermore, their care must be delivered with the comfort and compassion that is essential for them to accept it. Let me share my experience with you.

Examination and Treatment Planning

Start your relationship with your patient by spending time discussing their dental history, their past experiences, their current concerns and their potential roadblocks to treatment, be they emotional or financial. Understand where your patient is coming from and what their goals and expectations are for the future.

Once you have identified your patient's dental problems, explain these problems to your patient in a slow, non-threatening way, giving your patient as much time as they want to ask any questions. It is often helpful to ask a spouse or significant other to attend this meeting, not because your patient can't completely understand your recommendations, but as a second set of 'ears', one who also might have questions, or who can help reinforce your explanations after the patient has left the office.

Patients often have emotional roadblocks and may not always hear everything you say, and the person who comes with them will be able to fill in the pieces for them. Dentistry is often a costly undertaking, and it is better that the patient's spouse or significant other hears the cost of the treatment plan directly from you, as they can then associate the cost with the complexity of the treatment plan you have just explained and ask any questions they may have. If there are financial roadblocks to the treatment, you will get a better sense of that with both the patient and spouse together at the time you explain the treatment plan.

Your examination may have revealed a number of dental problems, and it is important to explain **all** of these problems to your patient. However, I would recommend focusing your initial treatment recommendations on only the most pressing problems, explaining that while the other problems exist, they can be monitored and treated as it becomes necessary. This will not only convey a thoughtful and measured approach to your patient's care (building trust in them, showing that you are not trying to take advantage of them), it will place their future treatment needs in a '**dental treatment savings account**,' or '**treatment bank**' for future use. While this will initially cause a shortfall in income, after 6-8 months, the procedures in the treatment savings account will start to come back out for the treatment that has been 'banked' for this patient and for other patients, and will be replaced with new deferred treatment that is placed into the treatment savings account. At that point there will be no further loss of income to the dentist, and he or she will start experiencing sustainable growth that is built on trust.

Long-term financial success with sustained growth has long been founded on the acquisition of increasing numbers of new patients and by maximizing the treatment on each of these patients. The ability to grow and prosper is predicated on the 'home run' philosophy. Each new patient who is introduced to a practice is given a treatment plan, which addresses his or her needs. Most of these patients come from other practices where these needs have not been identified or properly explained, or where the patient may have declined treatment if they were explained. Many of their untreated dental problems are in the absence of symptoms. Rather than respecting the dentist's comprehensive approach to their dental needs, the patient feels they are being taken advantage of or have been overwhelmed by the scope and complexity of the dental recommendations, and they are suspect of the dentist's motives and the real necessity of the recommended treatment.

This concept is worth repeating: **To create a foundation of trust and respect, the patient and the dentist would be best served by the dentist honestly and completely outlining the patient's treatment needs, prioritizing those needs, and suggesting the most immediate treatment to be addressed. The remaining treatment should be delayed to a later date.** In effect, the dentist is suggesting that a small percentage of the patient's needs be addressed immediately, and the remaining treatment needs are 'put in the bank.' This approach has a number of benefits…it tells that patient that you are taking a thoughtful and 'conservative' approach to their care, it builds trust into a new doctor-patient relationship, and it reinforces that dentist's diagnostic skills in the patient's eyes when symptom develop at a later time related to a treatment need previously diagnosed ('you warned me about that problem'). Most importantly, it makes treatment acceptance in the future much more likely, because it is based on previous education and understanding, and established trust. Growth is achieved by increased treatment acceptance over time, and the goodwill and trust established in your existing patient population. These patients also serve as ambassadors for your practice, encouraging their friends and family members to have the same experience they have had. The best referral base for your practice is a loyal and trusting patient who believes in your approach and respects your objectives and ethics. It works!

The money talk….

There is an old expression that the cost of dental treatment is half of what the dentist thinks it should be and twice the cost of what the patient thinks it should be. What is most important is that the cost should be fair for both the dentist and patient. For that to be true, patients need to understand that providing dental care has very high costs, which is what contributes to the fees that are charged. When a patient enters a hospital, they are charged by the hospital, for equipment expenses, instruments, medicaments, staff and space, and separately by the physicians for patient care. These expenses are often rolled directly into their medical insurance, so they don't fully appreciate the fees.

The dentist's office is the hospital and doctor all rolled into one, where the dentist pays all of the expenses. It is important that patients understand that the fees they are charged reflect the costs of equipment, instruments, staff, insurance, supplies and materials. In addition, equipment expenses have grown dramatically in recent years, as technology has become an integral part of good clinical care. Patients want the best care and need to be educated how all of these different areas contribute to the cost of that care.

On the reverse side, if you are going to charge a significant fee for treatment, you need to provide the quality of treatment that is reflected in your fee.... modern equipment, the finest materials, a well-educated and compensated congenial staff, the best technology available, and taking sufficient time with each patient to maintain a positive relationship. Patients will not want to pay for the difference if they can't see a difference.

Financial arrangements with patients must be forthright, honest and well documented. Offer patients two choices...payment at the time of service, or Care Credit or another third party credit service. Offering credit directly to your patients will make your office into a bank and will take up a lot of your staff's time. It is better to use your time and your staff's time more effectively and focus on improved patient care. You can still accept insurance assignment if you wish, and request payment of the difference directly from the patient, or from Care Credit. This approach leads to very few misunderstandings or financial conflicts.

Patients do not like surprises, whether it is a change in treatment or an additional cost. Be up front, be honest, be understanding and show a little compassion, without apologizing for what you do or what you charge.

Remember: ***The bitterness of poor quality lasts long after the sweetness of low cost is forgotten!***

How is a patient greeted when they walk into the office?

Positively greet the patient by name and inquire about their welfare. It is the first opportunity that you have that day to show your patient that you respect them, and to impress them with your personal approach. It helps to build a relationship with a new patient, and reinforce a relationship with an existing patient, so that when there is a problem down the line, the patient feels they have a 'friend' they can go to in the office. This gives them comfort and confidence, and it helps to resolve future problems in a way that creates a positive impression of your practice.

What is the condition of the reception area?

When a patient opens the door to your office, do they see old, worn furniture, disorderly seating, a dirty environment (used tissues or torn magazines sitting on a chair or lying on the floor), a poor choice of magazines, poor lighting creating a dingy environment, inadequate seating (the guide is 1½ seats per operatory), or just an unwelcoming environment? You might ask: 'Why does it matter…no money is earned in the waiting room, it is not a 'profit center.' It matters! It matters because a pretty, comfortable, clean and well-appointed reception area gives patients comfort and confidence. It reflects what is important to you and your staff and it says a lot about you. It also shows respect for them. Furthermore, a patient will never believe they are being treated in a clean operatory after sitting in a dirty waiting room. Your commitment to your patient needs to include every interaction with them, including how they are treated in your reception area. All staff members, whether it is the administrative staff adjacent to the reception area or the dental assistant or hygienist who seats the patient, should monitor the condition of the reception area throughout the day.

Are the magazines two years old? Do they have tattered or torn covers?

Contrary to popular opinion, patients do not want to read a two year old 'Golf' or 'Popular Mechanics' magazine with the name of the addressee torn off. Why should you care about how patients feel in your reception area?...because patients want to be shown respect. Spend a few dollars and put current, high quality magazines in your reception area (People, Time or Newsweek, Sports Illustrated, Town and Country, Architectural Digest, Vogue, etc.) and remove old copies every two weeks (donate them to a local hospital or nursing home – they will really appreciate it). This says to your patients: I care about your comfort while you are in my office! The more comfortable they are, the less stressed they are, and the less stressed they are, the smoother their treatment will go once they get to the operatory. The people receiving your used magazines will see your name and mention it to their friends and relatives, creating goodwill.

What is the cleanliness and maintenance of supplies in the patient bathroom?

The cleanliness of the patient bathroom reflects the cleanliness of the entire office and it is everyone's responsibility to make sure that it is clean and well stocked. Whether it is an assigned responsibility, a common responsibility or a rotating responsibility to monitor and maintain it, it must be someone's responsibility! It must be done and done right!

How is the telephone answered?

Answering the telephone in a dental office is more important than most people realize. The telephone is your lifeline to the outside world, and how you speak to callers can create a warm, positive, and ingratiating interaction, or it can be a negative influence on the goals of your practice.

- Answer the phone by identifying the name of your office and your name (Good morning, this is Dr. Jones' office, Rachel speaking).
- Speak slowly and clearly...when you say the same thing every time you answer the phone, it is so commonplace to you that you often say it very quickly

and slur all the words together, making it very difficult for the caller to understand you.
- When the caller identifies him/herself, the first question you ask is 'How are you today?" You want the caller to relate to you as a person, not just a problem that needs fixing. Wait for the answer to the question and have a conversation before getting to the reason for the call. Being polite and respectful is always appropriate. This approach should apply to all callers, not just patients.
- How can I help you today? Find out why the caller is calling and take responsibility for addressing the problem, either by personally resolving the problem, or by calling the person who can resolve it. Don't put it back on the caller to make another call to someone else...you take care of it! If it means referring the problem to another staff member, you seek out that staff member and have them work with the patient. If it means a conversation with the dentist, you explain it to the dentist and be sure that you or the dentist returns the patient's call. If it's a sales call, you treat the caller with respect and explain why you might not be interested in their product...you don't just say we're not interested and hang up. You want your office to be thought of in the community where people are shown respect.

What do you do when the telephone rings and a patient is standing in front of you trying to make an appointment?

You apologize to the patient standing in front of you and excuse yourself, so you can answer the phone. If the call requires anything more than a quick response, please ask the caller if you can call them back soon as you are finished working with the patient who is in the office. AND BE SURE TO CALL THEM BACK PROMPTLY! Show each party respect.

Does a staff member acknowledge patients sitting in the waiting room while they are waiting?

When a patent arrives at your office they should be personally greeted and engaged in conversation if at all possible. Always maintain the connection, the relationship. After they have been seated in the reception area for ten minutes, engage them in conversation at regular intervals if at all possible. They should not feel forgotten. Each minute they sit there will add to their anxiety, which will make their treatment in the operatory more stressful, not only for the patient, but also for the dentist and staff. Additional stress will cause faster metabolism of anesthetic and potentially increased pain to the patient.

Does a staff member advise a waiting patient that the doctor is running late, and give them a chance to reschedule?

If the dentist has not seen a patient within 15 minutes of their appointed time, the patient should be given the option to reschedule. This shows respect for the patient's time and does not allow their anxiety to grow. If a patient is seen long after their appointed time, not only will the patient experience added anxiety, it will add to the anxiety of the doctor and staff, knowing they will need to rush to get back on time. Their anxiety will also carry over to the treatment for the next patient. Good treatment rarely results from a rushed appointment.

Does the office show respect for the patient's time, or do they ask them to come in early and then keep them waiting?

It is important to carefully evaluate your schedule. It is very destructive to bring a patient in early and then have them wait. It says to the patient that only the dentist's time is important. Your motto should be: 'It's all about the patient."

Does the staff have personal conversations that the patients can hear, either in the operatory or waiting area?

Patients really don't care about the personal lives of the staff in your dental office. They don't care about who they dated last night, what's going on in their marriages, or anything else. They care about getting good treatment in a timely way and in a caring environment. Forcing them to listen your staff's conversation shows your patients a lack of respect.

Is the patient escorted to and from the treatment area?

Patients should not be allowed to wander around your office. It violates the privacy of your other patients and exposes them to potential hazards or things that are counterproductive to their comfort or confidence. Patients should be escorted to the particular operatory where they are going, and then escorted back to the front desk upon completion of their treatment.

Is the patient left unattended for a significant period of time in the operatory?

If a patient is seated in an operatory for a significant period of time before treatment is undertaken, it shows a lack of respect for the patient's time, just as if they were left in the reception area for a long time. Furthermore, sitting in an operatory alone waiting to be treated is anxiety producing, which makes it hard for the patient, and stressful for the dentist and staff when they finally get around to the appointment. Don't park your patient in an operatory to make them think they are not still waiting for you. Don't do it!

Do the dentist and staff focus on the patient when they are in the operatory, or are they concerned about personal things or the need to run to another operatory or answer a telephone call?

When a dentist and staff member have worked together for a long time, particularly in the close, almost intimate, environment of the dental office, they develop a very close relationship. This is very natural, particularly when the assistant must be so in tune with the dentist that he/she must anticipate the dentist's needs to be appropriately prepared. When this type of close relationship exists, it takes a great deal of self-control on the part of both the dentist and staff to remember to avoid personal discussions in front of the patient. Forcing a patient to listen to a conversation when they have no alternative is a sign of disrespect.

Is the patient's comfort foremost in the minds of the doctor and staff while the patient is in the office?

Again, 'It's all about the patient!" Every aspect of the patient's time in your office should be about showing the patient respect, treating them with skill and compassion, and focusing on their comfort.

Are only the finest materials being used for each patient?

Or another way to put this, are you cutting corners and

using cheaper materials to save a few dollars. How will this less favorable material affect the accuracy and effectiveness of your treatment? Will it mean the restoration will not be as good, forcing it to be replaced prematurely? Will it mean the restoration will only last 4 years instead of 10? Remembering that a patient's anxiety at the dentist is partially a product of their overall dental experience, and that needing dental treatment more frequently as a result of a failing restoration will add to that anxiety, it is important that we do everything as well as we possibly can to maximize the longevity of the treatment we provide. This means we should spend the money to use only the best materials available.

The art of delivering anesthesia-

Administering a local anesthetic for a patient is integral to being able to provide quality dental care. Yet it is often treated as a necessary formality and rarely given the time and attention it deserves.

Don't ever provide dental treatment without adequate anesthesia! It hurts! It raises the patient's anxiety level and blood pressure! It creates more tension and stress for the dentist and assistant each time the patient moves, or winces, or complains of pain! It often encourages the dentist to rush to limit the patient's discomfort, thereby impacting the quality and accuracy of the procedure! You think that you are only hurting the patient for a minute or two, and then it will be over. **In reality,**

you are affecting their dental care for the rest of their life! You will create stress and anxiety, making it less likely that they will seek future dental care, as well as less likely that they will accept future treatment recommendations when they are forced to seek that care. As a result of your behavior, it will make it more likely that future dental problems will be more complex because care was delayed.

I have very successfully used the following techniques when administering anesthesia:

1. Ask the patient to take a deep breath just as the needle is piercing the mucosa.... this is a diversion, which forces them to think about something else because taking a deep breath is a conscious process.
2. Initially, give a small amount of anesthetic with the initial injection.
3. Wait a couple of minutes for that to take hold, and then insert the needle into the area already anesthetized and advance the anesthesia to the next area. Keep doing this over a period of time to slowly advance the anesthetic.
4. When giving a palatal injection, initially keep pressure on the injection site with your finger or the end of a mirror handle. Then, insert the needle for a fraction of a second (while the patient is taking a deep breath), administer a tiny bit of anesthetic and then quickly remove the needle. In and out -it

is over almost before the patient knows it. When the initial numbness takes hold, reinsert the needle and deliver the bolus of anesthetic to provide complete anesthesia. There will be no pain associated with this.
5. Go slowly and deliberately, always remembering there is a person on the other end of the needle. I would often take 10 minutes or more to progressively anesthetize a patient.
6. Give the anesthetic time to work. If the patient is not completely anesthetized, deliver more anesthetic.
7. If, after multiple injections, you have not achieved the desired level of anesthesia, reschedule the patient. If you go ahead and treat the patient when they are not fully anesthetized, you are causing them pain, creating stress, and jeopardizing any future relationship you will have with the patient. You are also further sensitizing the patient's anxiety and fear of dentistry!

Do the dentist and staff show patience and understanding when patients are having a difficult time during treatment, or are they annoyed because it's taking longer to treat the patient and making them late for their next patient?

Dentistry is hard. It is stressful and anxiety producing for patients, doctors and staff. It is easy to get frustrated when patients move, or produce too much saliva, or can't open their mouths wide enough so we can see what we're doing. These are not the patient's fault...they are really trying the best they possibly can. It is also frustrating when cement isn't setting quite right, or we can't quite get the perfect margin we were striving for. None of these frustrations can be solved by becoming annoyed, rushing or taking out our frustrations on the patient or staff member. Take a step back and do the right thing...whether that means rescheduling your next patient or rescheduling the patient you are working on to another day. Do the job right! Do what is in your patient's best interest! Do what will truly reflect positively on your practice and yourself! Treat your patient the way you would like to be treated.

Are short cuts avoided?

We are often presented with short cuts. If they potentially reflect adversely on the quality or longevity of the patient's care, the patient's comfort, or the respect of your staff, don't take them. They will end up costing you much more than what you will save.

Are patients treated without rushing or the use of excessive force? (Excessive force should be avoided in dentistry...that is how things break or patients, dentists and staff are injured.)

There is no place for excessive force in dentistry. If a crown doesn't fit, forcing it into place will not make it fit.

If, during an extraction, a tooth does not come out easily with reasonable force, additional methods such as bone removal or sectioning the tooth may be indicated to facilitate the extraction. Adding additional force alone will only lead to breakage of the tooth or the bone (or the jaw, for that matter). Technique and finesse are much more powerful tools than added force.

Above all, are the dentists, patients and staff always treated with respect?

Dentists must respect their patients, and this should be the fundamental foundation of their practice. Dentists must train their staff appropriately and respect not only their efforts, but also their time and commitment. Staff must respect the dentist(s) they work for, and their respect must have as its foundation honest behavior on the part of the dentist. If a dentist is perceived to be dishonest with their patients or staff, their staff may obey them but will never respect them. Without that respect, there will always be a chasm between the dentist and staff members, which will reflect on the atmosphere in the office and the stress level. Patients can sense when there is stress in an office because they are usually under stress to begin with, and a stressful environment only accentuates what they are already feeling. It's all about respect.

How does clinical treatment impact patient trust?

First and foremost, does the treatment address the problem it is meant to address and is it successful? If the treatment does not satisfactorily resolve a problem, then the diagnosis was wrong or the treatment was wrong or performed in a less than favorable way. Patients have the rightful expectation that their problems be fully explained to them so they can make a truly informed consent to have treatment. They then have the further expectation that their treatment will be performed to the highest standards. Finally, they have the logical expectation that the treatment will solve their problem. If their clinical problem remains after treatment is completed, or if we know that the diagnosis was inadequate or the treatment inappropriate, we must be honest with patients immediately and inform them about what is going on.

While we often take a great deal of pride in our clinical skills or treatment outcomes, patients care about how long a procedure takes, how much pain is involved, whether or not their problem has been solved, how much the procedure costs, and what post-treatment or post-operative instructions are important. As a periodontist, I have found that there are a number of ways to minimize patient discomfort or disfiguration, and these have a significant influence on patient trust.

Anesthesia: As outlined above, anesthesia should be administered in a slow, deliberate and gentle way, to reduce patient anxiety and increase trust.

Surgical procedures should be designed to minimize trauma, which will minimize swelling and pain. Examples:

1. Do minimal flap elevation at the outset of a procedure, only to the crest of bone, and then only do additional elevation for access for the briefest period of time to accomplish your treatment objectives when you are ready to address a particular clinical problem. In this way, bone is minimally exposed which will have a direct affect on patient comfort.
2. Try to avoid vertical releasing incisions unless they are absolutely necessary for access, and then only make that incision when you are ready to elevate that tissue to get the access.
3. Work quickly and efficiently to try to minimize the time of bone exposure.
4. Use only the best materials.
5. When doing a free gingival graft, always suture the donor site, the apical border of the graft and the coronal border of the reflected recipient site tissue. This will minimize bleeding, minimize swelling, and minimize pain.
6. Tie sutures so that the knots are inaccessible to the tongue. This eliminates a source of annoyance for the patient and helps to prevent the sutures from becoming prematurely loose.
7. If you use a dressing to cover a free gingival graft, consider using Barricade, which is pink, so the

patient will not have periodontal dressing showing when they smile.
8. Even if post-operative instructions are printed, take the time to review them chairside, emphasizing the use of ice to limit swelling.
9. Be sure the patient has your cell phone number so you can be reached. I have found over many years that patients will very rarely abuse the privilege of being able to call you, but will have much less post-operative anxiety just knowing that they can reach you if they have to.
10. Always call your patient the evening after a surgical procedure. Firstly, it shows the patient that you care. Secondly, it shows that you really do want to know about a problem if one exists. Thirdly, patients will often have questions they forgot to ask in the office or which they consider too trivial to bother calling you over. Answering these questions puts their minds at ease…less anxiety makes for less pain. Fourthly, you have to double check that your patient is taking their medication as instructed, something they are often confused about. Lastly, it will alert you to a developing problem, which is easily treated before it becomes more serious.

Relationships with Staff

Dental staff members are an essential part of the equation of good care, patient comfort, personal satisfaction and professional fulfillment. A practice must establish standards and goals, effective practices and professional guidelines and staff members need to be fully trained and educated in order to not only respect and reflect those practices, but also to find happiness and job satisfaction in their pursuit.

Dentistry is a precise and exacting profession, often practiced in a very stressful environment. There are different personality types, and not every personality might be best suited for employment in a dental practice. Furthermore, the personality type of a prospective employee must also be evaluated in light of the personalities of the staff that already exists. Will they complement those already there or create conflicts? There must be a harmonious group of people whose skills and motivation reflect the mission and goals of the practice, and who facilitate its growth and success.

Every aspect of a dental practice must be evaluated by the following standard:

Is it about the patient? Where you went on your date last night is not about the patient. What time you need to pick up your child from child-care is not about the patient. What you should wear to a party next weekend is not about the patient. It is normal for people who work closely together to want to have these discussions…have them on the phone outside of work, or at lunchtime sitting around in the staff room. Do not have them while you're in the operatory or chatting with a staff member in the sterilizing area or lab.

Training a staff is the dentist's responsibility, as it is impossible to achieve a high standard of patient care and a harmonious and fulfilling work environment without it. Above all, staff members must be treated with respect and honesty. If the dentist running the practice is dishonest, the staff will know. They will never respect the dentist and there will always be a stressful work environment. Dishonesty comes in many forms...it could mean stealing cash rather than depositing it and accounting for it, it could mean using a cheaper material when a better one is available, it could mean cutting corners and giving patients less than ideal treatment, it could mean being disrespectful to patients and treating them poorly, it could mean providing recommendations or providing treatment that isn't really necessary. No dentist will engender the cooperation and respect of his/her staff with this type of behavior. If the staff believes that the dentist is not putting the patient first, they will not put the patient first. The dentist must be honest, compassionate, fair and competent.... he or she must lead by example. Striving for excellence will always be respected...it will excite your staff and make them feel that they are part of something that is bigger than themselves.

Even under the best of circumstances, when a group of people are always striving for perfection and working in close quarters in a stressful environment, frustrations and conflicts will occur. It is important that dentists manage their staff fairly, without showing favorites, and address whatever problem exists **promptly and decisively.** Every action should be evaluated first by asking: Is it about the patient? If not, it has no place in the office. If it is about the patient, then the answer almost always lies in how the dentist and staff can best address the patient's care, whether it's about treatment quality, patient comfort or respectful interaction between patient, doctor and staff.

There are two big mistakes that dentists make with respect to staff. The first is when they join a practice as an employee, or associate. They try to become friends with the staff, often because they see themselves as another employee similar to the hygienist or the assistant. You are not their friend! You may one day become their employer and you will create roadblocks that make it very difficult to ultimately retain the same staff. The other big mistake is that dentists develop personal relationships with the staff members. This has multiple problems associated with it:

- It will ruin your family and their family
- It will poison your relationship with the rest of your staff and the relationships the staff members have with each other
- It will make you susceptible to legal action

Dentistry is a very intimate profession by its very nature…. we work inches from another person's body, we touch tissues which are very sensitive, we work on a part of the body responsible for kissing, talking, laughing, eating and being the primary expression of human interaction. Don't let the intimacy inherent in our work carry over to an intimate relationship with your staff.

I have worked in two practices, one for 32 years and the second for 10 years. In the first practice I had 2 hygienists and 2 assistants who worked for me for 25 years, another hygienist and assistant who worked for me for more than 10 years. In my second practice, I had an assistant and office administrator that worked for me for almost 10 years. All of these people are individuals who I feel close to, to this day. I value them, I respect them, I am enormously fond of them, and most of all, I am thankful that we had the opportunity to work together, because they allowed me to achieve my practice goals, deliver wonderful care to my patients, and made me feel like I was working with my extended family every day. I could never have had the same professional accomplishments or personal satisfaction without them. When you leave the office at the end of the day, say 'thank you' to your staff. Don't forget, even for one day. **And mean it!**

Some dental offices have different strata of employees, with hygienists ranking at the top, then assistants and then a different stratum for administrative staff. In my office, all of the employees were equal…. they had different duties, but each shared an equal responsibility to create the best possible treatment in the most caring environment for each patient. For each of them, it was their office as much as it was mine.

Retaining a long-term staff, particularly one, which can work in a harmonious and productive environment, will give your patients much comfort, reduce their anxiety and encourage them to trust your treatment recommendations and proceed with necessary treatment. They will reinforce your treatment goals and create the atmosphere where your patients feel comfortable and reassured in accepting them.

The Office Manager

Many offices, particularly larger practices, employ an office manager. Is his or her role to manage all facets of the practice? Is the primary role to manage employees? Is his or her primary role to separate employee issues from the dentist and act as a buffer when there are employee complaints? In my 42 years of practice, I never had an office manager, even when I had 10 employees. I wanted my employees to feel they had access to me when they had concerns or complaints. I felt they were like family members and I didn't want a degree of separation from them, any more than I would from my children or spouse. I was fortunate to have exceptional staff loyalty and longevity. There is nothing wrong with having an office manager, but his or her job should not be to protect the dentist. The office manager should encourage and foster interaction between the dentist and the employees in the office.

Relationships with Colleagues

Dentistry is a hard, exacting and demanding profession. We work with limited visibility on an anxious patient where the success of our treatment may depend on how wide a patient can open his/her mouth as much as it does our skill. Other than your dental assistant, nobody knows what goes on in your patient's mouth while you are treating them...it's easy to keep a secret if something doesn't go quite right. Moreover, we are often suspect? jealous? wary? of other dentists in our community if they saw the patient before we did, or if they might see the patient after us and comment on our work. To begin with, it's hard enough for the patient to trust the dental profession, and this only makes it that much harder. I would like to suggest that this is entirely the wrong approach.

Every dentist understands how hard dentistry is. We are all in the same boat, we have had the same experiences, we all work under similar conditions, we all share the same frustrations and challenges and we have many of the same feelings about each other. It is time for dentists to treat each other as colleagues, not competitors, as co-therapists, not critics.

Dentists should start off by talking to other dentists in their community, share frustrating problems, and ask for their advice and guidance. Physicians have access to hospital review boards and grand rounds to share their practice problems. Dentists are solo acts, working individually, with the option to keep their problems and shortcomings in the closet. It is time to share our experiences and have the dentists in our community come together to serve as an educational resource for each other. Not only will we grow and learn, we will feel less alone and more comforted that there are others who are having the same problems we are. As a result of being part of a community of dentists, we will learn, we will grow, we will better serve our patients and we will find much more happiness and fulfillment in our work. There are enough patients for everybody and they will ultimately determine who they feel most comfortable looking after them.

Relationships in your Community

None of us practices in a vacuum. We live in a community, our patients live in that community, our staff lives in that community and our colleagues live in that community.

Our relationship with our communities can serve as a positive influence on our practices, as long as it is not at the expense of colleagues. Advertising that you are the best implies that your colleagues are not as good as you…. advertise your services if you wish, but it is best not to compare yourself with others.

Be a positive influence in your community, whether in community service, participating in community organizations or events, or at your place of worship. Do things outside of dentistry that will benefit those where you live and give people in the community an opportunity to get to know you as a person, not a dentist. I can assure you they will make the connection when the need to see a dentist arises in their life.

To help build better relationships in your community, you can also work with your local dental society to contribute and help make your community a better place. Goodwill towards dentists as individuals and dentistry as a profession can only improve your practice and create positive feelings towards your profession.

Relationships with Dental Suppliers

When a representative from a dental supplier or manufacturer appears in your waiting room, you may consider this an inconvenience and a waste of your time, particularly if you have no interest in the product they are representing.

Whenever I was confronted with that situation, I would go out to the waiting room, greet the rep and thank them for stopping by. Why would I do that if I had no interest in what they were selling?

Let me tell you – it's called polite and respectful behavior. Your dental reps are people first! It is not easy being a rep, it is not easy to be turned away and rejected. Reps have feelings, they have families, and they interact with many reps from other companies. Do you want a reputation as being a kind and considerate human being who relates to people? Or would you like to be known as someone who doesn't care about others, someone who thinks their time is so important that the people who are trying to help them don't matter.

Professional goodwill is something you should try to establish with every person in your professional life... goodwill with your dental suppliers is just as important as goodwill with your patients. Your rep is also a patient; the reps he or she talks to are also patients. Behave in a manner that demonstrates that your rep is a person who deserves your respect, even if you choose not to use their product. That extra 30 seconds it costs you to say hello will serve you well.

When you attend a dental meeting, be kind and courteous to the dental reps that are staffing the different booths. Try staffing a booth for a day and see how hard a job it is.... it's exhausting.

Many dentists I know essentially 'use' dental reps. Instead of establishing an honest and productive relationship with a rep, they shop from company to company until they can save a couple of bucks. I would suggest that your time would be better spent by developing a trusting, respectful and honest relationship with your rep and let them help you grow and flourish. I can tell you the dental reps I have worked with during my career have bent over backwards to help my practice. With an established and trusting relationship, they always gave me favorable pricing, they were there when there was a problem, they served as ambassadors of goodwill in my community, and they went out of their way to work hard for me, so that I could be the best I could be.

Relationships with Specialists

As a periodontist, I can tell you that relationships with dentists and other specialists in the community can be very complex. Let us explore these different relationships.

The most important thing to remember is that your patient becomes a **mutual** patient. It is so important that your communication reflects multiple providers of care, not only for patient comfort and confidence, but also, so that there is no confusion about the treatment and that it is completed accurately. It is often helpful to include the patient in communication between the various providers of care. It serves as a reinforcement of the treatment objectives that were explained to the patient and gives the patient confidence that the various providers caring for them are **working together**.

If you are a general dentist, don't insult a specialist by thinking that you can do a procedure just as well as he or she can. I'm not saying you shouldn't do these procedures. If you want to do endo, or perio, or place an implant, and you have the necessary training and experience, and you can do a good job for your patient, by all means, treat your patients with these procedures. And enjoy doing so. But it is delusional to think that if you spend 3% of your time doing endo, that you are going to do it as well or expeditiously as a specialist who spends 100% of their time doing endo. It is just not logical to think that by placing 50 implants a year that you are as skillful as someone who places 500 implants per year. If you were the patient, which clinician would you like treating you? The additional training and the countless hours of experience do make a difference…. in 'Outliers', Malcolm Gladwell states that you need to do something for 10,000 hours before you become really good at. Having said that, it is important that specialists and general dentists exhibit mutual respect.

For the general dentist:

- Recognize that the specialist has years of additional training and countless hours of additional experience, and that this will contribute to a positive result and benefit for **your patient**
- Do not **use** the specialist, such as consulting on a case and then treating the patient yourself
- Work to develop a positive and trusting relationship with the specialist; it will make the referral process second nature, and it will make it easier for the specialist to refer patients to you
- Provide detailed and well documented information to the specialist to make it easier to treat **your** patient
- Be honest with the specialist. If you are planning to treat certain types of patients that require that kind of specialty care, ask the specialist where to get the best training so you can do the best possible job for your patient. You might also want to establish a framework for referrals, so the specialist will know that while you are providing some treatment within the specialty, there are other types of cases you are going to defer to the specialist

For the specialist:

- Recognize that the general dentist is going to treat some of the patients that fall within your specialty
- Help to educate the general dentist as to the types of cases he or she should or should not treat
- Work with the general dentist to help make them as good as they can be, and establish a referral framework for the types of cases that fall outside those parameters
- Communicate in a positive and respectful way, always recognizing that you are sharing in the care of a mutual patient

Specialist to specialist:

- If a patient requires the care of multiple specialists, there are now at least four people in the relationship —each specialist, the general dentist and the patient
- Be sure that all communication regarding the patient's needs includes everyone in this relationship, including the patient. It will build confidence and help insure the accuracy of the treatment.

Most of all...
Make it about what is best for the patient, not keeping the patient in your office for additional income!

How Can a Specialist Create a Productive Referral Base?

- Make yourself a predictable and reliable resource for the general dentists and other specialists in your community
- Always be available to accommodate the needs of your referral base, even if it means working through lunch or after hours. The ability to do this impacts your relationship with your staff…. if they respect you and what you are trying to achieve, they will be more than willing to help.
- Educate the general dentist about what you can offer his or her patients. Invite the generalist to your office to observe procedures, particularly on mutual patients.
- Whenever you see a patient, comment on their relationship with their general dentist to reinforce that relationship and the mutual relationship with you. When you see a new patient, say 'I see you are a patient of Dr. Jones, she is a wonderful dentist and you are fortunate to have her looking after you.' This reassures the patient that their choice in a general dentist is sound and that the two of you will work well together.
- Schedule lunch and learn sessions in the generalist's office, so the staff can also learn about what you can offer. Patients rely on the staff for their opinions and recommendations
- Plan joint social functions between your two offices,

so the staff can get to know each other. It is much easier to schedule a referral if both administrative staffs know each other. It is much easier and comforting for patients if the clinical staff knows the clinical staff in the other office
- Develop a non-clinical relationship with your referring dentists...golf, an investment club, social plans with spouses, trips together, attending educational forums together, etc.

Bigger is better?

There is a common belief that having a bigger office, with more operatories and a larger staff is more productive and more profitable. I would contend that this is not necessarily true.

My first practice involved two practice locations (6 operatories in one, 3 in the second), a periodontist partner and ten employees and I practiced in that environment for 32 years. My second practice was a solo practice with two operatories and two employees. One would naturally think that the first, larger practice was more symbolic of 'success', more productive, more profitable and more enjoyable. Not true!

The larger practice, particularly with multiple locations, has a larger overhead...more equipment, more rent, more insurance, more maintenance, more IT ramifications, and more staff.... which means more salaries, benefits, conflicts, and much more time spent on management. Having a large staff and a partner is far more stressful than having a 2-person staff and a solo practice. I can tell you, having practiced both ways that bigger is not necessarily better. In my second practice, I was equally productive but much more profitable, as my overhead was greatly reduced. I chose to spend a great deal of time with my patients instead of running from room to room, which helped me build lasting, trusting relationships, and improved case acceptance. It gave me a great deal of enjoyment and satisfaction. I would think that everyone's goal should be to enhance your income and reduce your stress, while providing excellent clinical care to a patient who trusts and respects you.

I can assure you…both types of practices have their plusses and minuses, but bigger is not necessarily better.

Striving for excellence

The pursuit of excellence in dentistry should be the foundation of every dental practice. Dentistry is not easy. We work in a small, restricted space, with limited visibility and access. Our patients are, for the most part, fully awake and therefore move their heads or tongues or produce excess saliva while we work on them, creating a host of challenges. Most patients have the emotional baggage of their previous dental experiences, and this often creates an emotionally charged environment. We physically work 1-2 inches from our patient's faces…. we are invading their 'space.' We also work in very close proximity to our staff. Through all of this, we are expected to deliver precise, accurate, artistic dental treatment in the absence of any pain or discomfort. Not so easy...

How can we maintain our goals of dental excellence in this environment while minimizing the challenges and limiting stress? First, we need to have our patient's trust and cooperation, and that has to be earned before we set out to treat them. The trust is built by spending time with patients, talking to them, educating them, reassuring them, and trying not to overwhelm them with the immediate need to treat all of their dental problems. We need to spend the time with our patients and develop a personalized relationship.

As mentioned earlier, we should use techniques to anesthetize our patients that reduce trauma and pain.... using a topical anesthetic, injecting very slowly, progressively injecting non-anesthetized areas by going through areas already anesthetized. In addition to the topical anesthetic, ask your patient to take a deep breath while administering the initial injection. They will be less likely to feel it. Most importantly, take as much time as necessary and go slowly. You should be thinking only about that patient while you are giving the injections, not the patient you are in the middle of treating in the next room or the two hygienists waiting for you.

Treat one patient at time.

This is one of the most important aspects of improving

patient trust, reducing stress and maintaining excellence. If you are thinking about something other than the patient in front of you, you are not focusing on that patient's needs and you will be more likely to rush, causing them pain or creating a stressful environment. Focus only on the patient you are with and spend the time that is necessary to do the best possible job in the most comforting way. If you rush, the patient will feel more insecure. The stress will affect you, the patient and your staff, and the quality of your work will suffer. You want your patient to trust and respect you...you need to show them that you respect them!

Everything matters!

Consider the office that took great pride in their commitment to infection control. They worked on infection control training, they established the recommended infection control systems and they advertised that they were committed to only the highest standards of infections control. But the staff didn't really take pride in the office. One of the patients dropped a tissue on the floor in the hallway or left a magazine under a chair in the reception area. Each staff member didn't think it was his or her job to pick it up. So, the tissue and the magazine sat there. And every patient who walked through the office saw them. And in spite of their training and proclamations attesting to their commitment to only the highest standards of infection control, every patient that day thought the office was dirty. You can spend a great deal of time and energy trying to do it right. But one small failing can undo all of your efforts. Everything matters! You and your staff must treat your office like it is your home, taking pride in its appearance and cleanliness.

In today's world of social media and internet posts, patients are free to 'rate' you all the time. If you are honest and genuine and try to focus on the right way of doing things, it will lead to positive, not negative, comments.

Everything really does matter. If your office is sparkling clean, but you are rushed and don't pay attention to your patients, it will create a negative image. If you pay attention to your patient, but are abrupt and rude to your staff, it will create a negative image. If you provide great care but keep patients waiting a long time, it will create a negative image. Dentists are famous for trying hard but shooting themselves in the foot for not paying attention to everything. It all matters.

Practice Transitions

A private practice is often purchased by a younger dentist, who may be a recent graduate, or a dentist with some experience in practice. Almost invariably, however, the dentist purchasing the practice will have little or no practice management experience. It is a very exciting time for the purchaser, but also one filled with potential roadblocks to success:

Goodwill – in addition to the physical assets of the

practice, the incoming dentist is purchasing the goodwill of the retiring dentist. As he or she begins to meet and evaluate the patients in the practice, the incoming dentist may find work that is not up to their standards, or treatment needs that have not been addressed. It requires excellent communication skills and an understanding of long-term goals to explain the treatment needs to their new patient without alienating them and losing the goodwill they have so dearly paid for. It will also help to preserve the positive relationship the patient has with the retiring dentist and protect them from potential legal repercussions.

Staff – retaining the existing staff can be a significant benefit in patient retention, as the patients are familiar with them and used to seeing them in that particular office. The existing staff can also help make the patients they know so well more comfortable with the new dentist. However, the staff will have an underlying loyalty to the retiring dentist and will be used to doing things in a way that may not be comfortable or productive for the incoming dentist. It requires excellent communication skills and people skills to reorient the staff to their new employer to help make the transition easier and preserve goodwill.

Many practices are purchased with the help of brokers, who do an excellent job of matching the needs of both parties in the sale of the practice. However, it is not their job or their skill set to provide support after the sale is completed. Even though the incoming dentist has just invested a great deal in purchasing the practice, he or she should consider an experienced practice coach to help navigate the goodwill and staff issues in the new office. The new dentist will be reluctant to spend money on a practice coach after having made a major investment to purchase the practice. However, the relatively small amount that he or she will pay for this service will not only help to preserve the existing goodwill, it will lay the foundation for a productive and successful practice in the future. Failing to do so is like purchasing a sophisticated piece of machinery without investing in the necessary training to make it work in the most efficient way. Most incoming dentists will think that they already know what needs to be done; they should remember: 'You don't know what you don't know!' It is too late after the patient feels alienated and leaves the practice…the goodwill is lost.

Honesty

Honesty is the very basis of how you should practice and live your life. You should be honest with your patients, your staff, your colleagues, and of course, your family. Most importantly, you should be honest with yourself. You don't know what you don't know. Don't do a procedure unless you are knowledgeable and skillful at it. It may be tempting to earn the additional income. But this will be offset by the associated stress, the potential for failure, and both you and ultimately the patient knowing that you really didn't do such a good job. Take the time to invest in ongoing educational opportunities, not because you need so many hours to renew your license, but because it will make you a better dentist and allow you to deliver the highest quality of care to your patients. Materials change, equipment changes, techniques change, and concepts evolve. If you don't change and evolve with your profession, you will do a disservice to your patients and you will limit your growth opportunities as a professional and as a person.

Internal Marketing

Internal Marketing involves addressing your existing patient base. To help them appreciate what you do, and make them ambassadors for your practice (creating and encouraging goodwill amongst their family and friends), think about the following:

- create the most positive experience in your office when they are there – how they are treated by the clinical and administrative staff, how they are treated by you (are they the sole focus of your attention when they are there?), take the time to address their needs – don't rush!
- does your office reflect the clinical standards you are trying to achieve? Did you treat your patient honestly and fairly? Did you use good communication

skills to explain treatment needs and expenses? Did you take the time to listen to your patient's concerns?
- each time a patient is in your office, it is an opportunity for you and your staff to impress them with your attention, skill, kindness, caring, compassion and understanding.
- when a patient completes treatment in your office, do an 'exit' interview' – ask them about their experience in your office. If their experience is unfavorable in some way, address it and find out how is can be corrected. If their experience is favorable, have a preprinted card available with a web address where they can make a positive comment on your website about their experience in your office.
- As mentioned before, everything matters, and when you do it right, patients will notice and will be more than willing to tell their friends and family members. As they say, -why pay the difference if you can't tell the difference.

Expectations

It is important to have realistic expectations. It is very tempting to think you know it all when you graduate from dental school, when in fact, you are just beginning your education. Be humble, you will make mistakes and you will learn from them, just like everyone else. Be an optimist. An optimist sees the opportunity in every difficulty;

a pessimist sees the difficulty in every opportunity. It is important to have professional goals and it is also important to have professional role models. But don't think for a minute that your role models didn't make mistakes as they travelled their road of professional growth. What is important is to learn from those mistakes.

It is also important to have realistic financial expectations. Dentistry is a wonderful profession with the opportunity to earn a handsome living, but it is something that takes time. Keep to your path without sacrificing your goals, and you will get there.

If this handbook could be summarized in 5 words: **It's all about the patient!**

www.ingramcontent.com/pod-product-compliance
Lightning Source LLC
Chambersburg PA
CBHW050025230526
45470CB00003B/1134